Walking in Winter on the Camino
A Pilgrimage on the Camino de Santiago

Brian Morrison

Walking in Winter
on the Camino
A Pilgrimage on the
Camino de Santiago

© 2018 Brian Morrison
All Rights Reserved

TEXT AND PHOTOS BY:
Brian Morrison

PUBLISHED BY
BRIAN MORRISON
Albuquerque, NM
www.brianscamino.com

Trade Paperback ISBN:
978-0-692-11240-3

ebook ISBN:
978-0-692-11513-8

Library of Congress
Control Number:
2018905102

116 pages, 59 photos

Travel • Spiritual • Fitness

DESIGN: Charlie Kenesson,
Kenesson Design, Inc.

Table of Contents

Acknowledgments iv
Introduction 1
28 Days on Camino Frances—Stages 5
My Winter Pilgrimage 9
Interview with a Winter Pilgrim 43

The birth of an idea 44	Memorable encounters 67
A change of plans 45	Camino angels 68
Finishing what I started ... 46	Walking to O Cebreiro 69
Preparing 47	The last push 78
Busy season vs winter 50	The fall 82
January challenges 52	Arriving in Santiago 85
Albergues in winter 55	What to pack 89
Warm water 56	Reflections 98
Feelings and fears 57	Other things 103
Challenging sections 59	

Packing Checklist 107
Useful Phone Apps 111

Acknowledgments

My gratitude goes to Linnea Hendrickson for the interview. This book would not have been possible without her support and encouragement to write down my winter Camino experience.

My brother David for inspiring me to keep walking.

My sincere thanks to the wonderful people in Spain who pointed me in the right direction from time to time.

Introduction

Each year hundreds of thousands of pilgrims trek across Spain arriving at the cathedral at Santiago de Compostela where the tomb of the apostle of Saint James is located. As far back as the Middle Ages pilgrims have walked the way of Saint James often trekking hundreds of miles. The mountain ranges and formidable table lands of the Meseta are traversed by pilgrims on a journey through history as they walk along roads and bridges built by the Romans. Sometimes they begin their journey from the doorsteps of their homes in Europe and beyond. While others travel from overseas to begin their pilgrimage. The French Way, or Camino Frances, begins 500 miles from Santiago in the French town of Saint Jean Pied de Port. Modern day pilgrims begin the pilgrimage for different reasons, including spiritual enlightenment, religion, physical fitness and adventure. Today's pilgrims carry a special passport to collect stamps each day, which they present to receive the

Compostela certificate at the cathedral in Santiago de Compostela. The Compostela is written in Latin and recognizes the completion of the pilgrimage. The cathedral also provides a certificate for distance, which is a slightly larger document on parchment. I walked half the Camino with my brother David in the fall of 2016, and returned to finish the 500 mile, million step, journey in the winter of 2018. This is the story of my winter experience on the Camino.

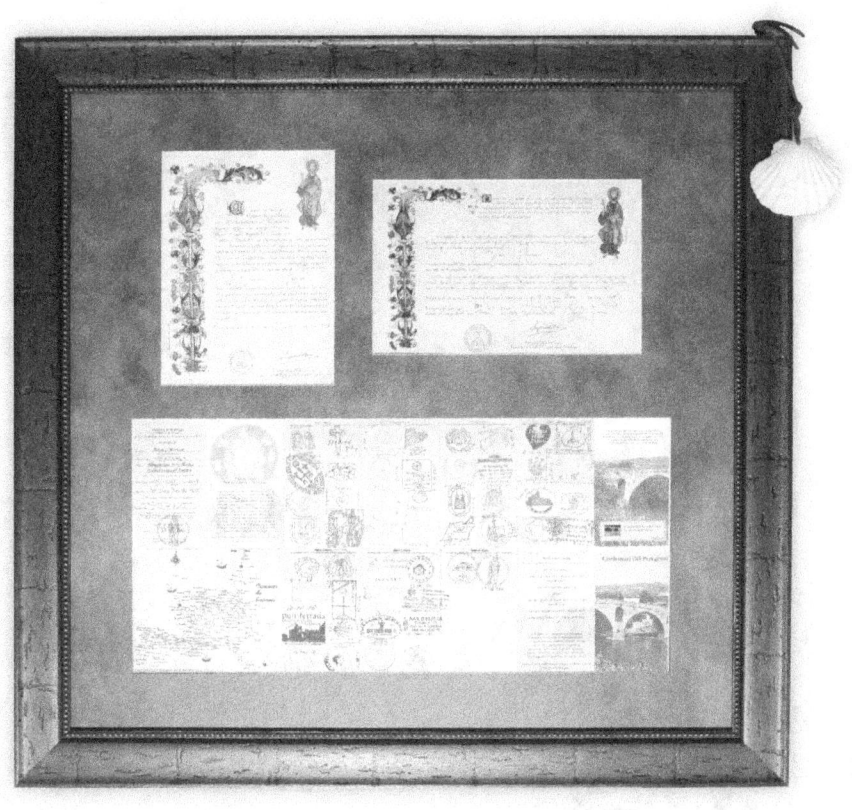

My framed Camino passport,
Compostela certificate, and distance certificate.

Approaching Cirauqui—taken on my walk with David in 2016

28 Days on Camino Frances—Stages

October 2016
My autumn walk with David

Day 1   Saint Jean Pied de Port to Roncesvalles
Day 2   Roncesvalles to Larrasoaña
Day 3   Larrasoaña to Cizur Menor
Day 4   Cizur Menor to Cirauqui
Day 5   Cirauqui to Villamayor de Monjardín
Day 6   Villamayor de Monjardín to Viana
Day 7   Viana to Nájera
Day 8   Nájera to Santo Domingo de la Calzada
Day 9   Santo Domingo de la Calzada to Belorado
Day 10   Belorado to Cardeñuela Riopico
Day 11   Cardeñuela Riopico to Burgos
Day 12   Burgos to León (via train)
Day 13   León to San Martín
Day 14   San Martín to Astorga

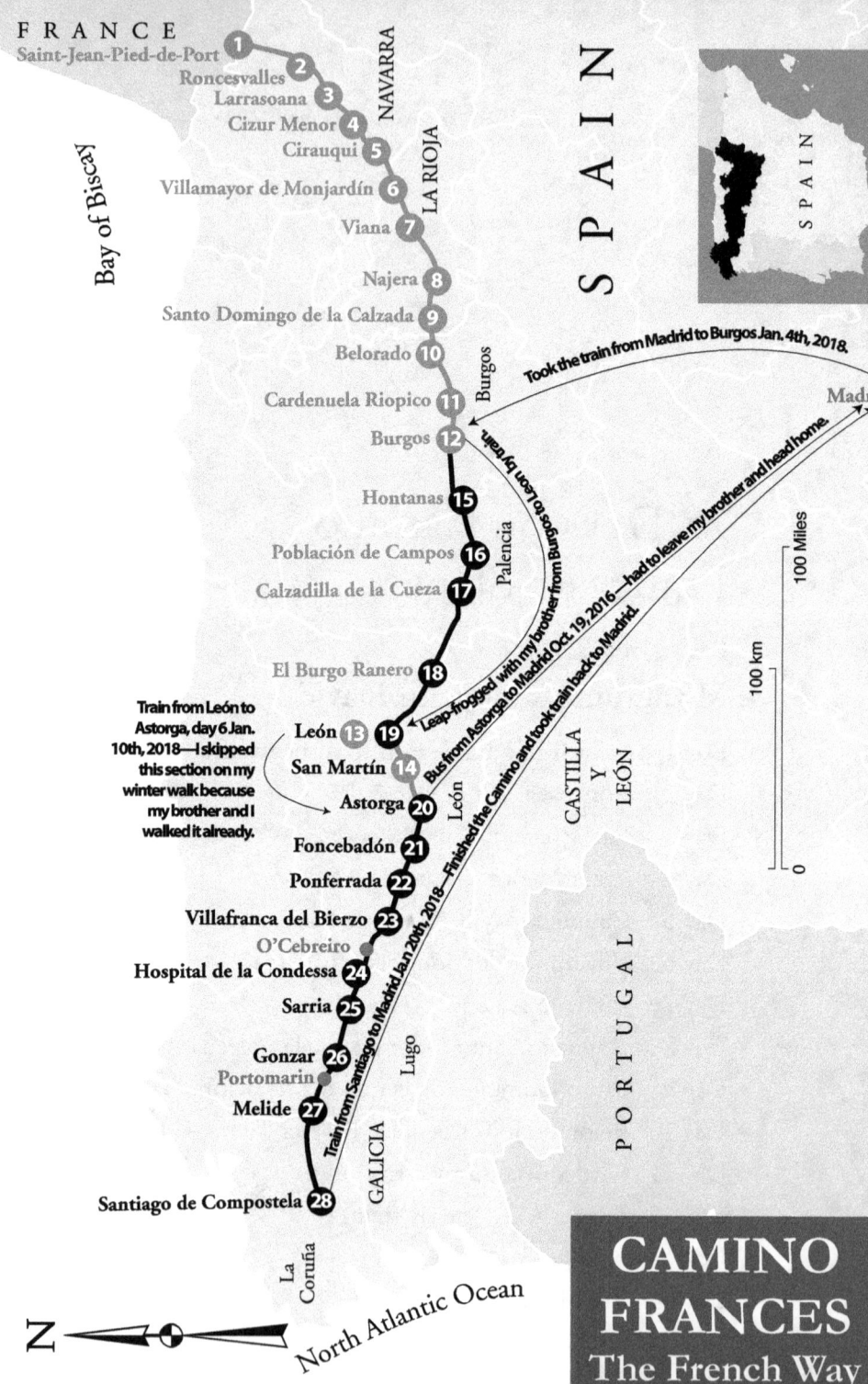

January 2018
My winter walk alone

Day 1 (15)	Burgos to Hontanas
Day 2 (16)	Hontanas to Poblacíon de Campos
Day 3 (17)	Poblacíon de Campos to Calzadilla de la Cueza
Day 4 (18)	Calzadilla de la Cueza to El Burgo Ranero
Day 5 (19)	El Burgo Ranero to León, Leon to Astorga (via train)
Day 6 (20)	Astorga to Foncebadón
Day 7 (21)	Foncebadón to Ponferrada
Day 8 (22)	Ponferrada (rest day)
Day 9 (23)	Ponferrada to Villafranca del Bierzo
Day 10 (24)	Villafranca del Bierzo to Hospital de la Condesa
Day 11 (25)	Hospital de la Condesa to Sarria
Day 12 (26)	Sarria to Gonzar
Day 13 (27)	Gonzar to Melide
Day 14 (28)	Melide to Santiago de Compostela

◀ Map of my Camino Frances. The gray numbered circles indicate the stops on my fall pilgrimage taken with my brother in 2016. The black numbered circles indicate the stops on my winter pilgrimage taken alone in 2018.

My Winter Pilgrimage

Daily updates posted on Facebook

The entries that follow are my day-by-day Facebook posts to family and friends on the second half of my journey. I tidied them up a little and used some of the photos in other places, but they are pretty much as they were when I walked. The photos are from the days I posted these entries.

January 3, 2018

On my way to Spain to complete my remaining 300-mile (482 km) pilgrimage on the Camino de Santiago.

◄ Pilgrim's shadow

January 4, 2018

Upon arriving in Burgos I checked into the two-story municipal albergue as two police officers were escorting a mentally deranged man from the foyer. Only pilgrims are allowed to stay in the 150-bed albergue after showing their pilgrim's passport. The man was trying to stay the night in the albergue without a pilgrim's passport and he refused to leave. There were only two other pilgrims staying that night.

I attended the evening pilgrim's mass at the enormous Gothic cathedral of Saint Mary of Burgos. I did not understand a single word. However, I felt blessed for the journey ahead of me. After eating a traditional Spanish dinner, including pincho de tortilla and ensalada Rusa, I returned to the albergue to sleep. The lights in the albergue were turned off at 11:00 p.m. It was time to sleep. Before falling asleep I wondered if the police would be in the albergue at 8:00 a.m. to check if the pilgrims were on their way.

Lesson learned today: I read a thread online that you may not have hot water in the albergues in winter. I learned the very first day in the Burgos municipal albergue that this is not necessarily the case. After traveling all the way from Madrid to Burgos my first shower was not warming up no matter how many times I pushed the button on the valve. I ended up grinning and bearing the cold water and I somehow got through the shower. Then, just before I finished rinsing off, the water started to warm up. I couldn't believe it! Beware of what you read online, because it might influence you to give up hope for a warm shower too early.

The first day started in cold rain.

Burgos-Hontanas—
It was cold, I caught up to the Korean pilgrim in distance

January 5, 2018 • Day 1 (15)
Burgos to Hontanas

I departed the Burgos albergue before sunrise at 7:30 and walked to the edge of town. The first 10 miles of the Meseta were cold, windy and raining. My fleece gloves were the first of several equipment items to fail me. They became soaked and had to be removed. I was cold and wet under my rain gear and not sure if my sweat was propagating out through the layers of clothing or if the rain was coming in. That afternoon the rain let up and I started to dry out. I met another pilgrim from South Korea a few miles from Hontanas. We both arrived at the Hontanas municipal albergue and called the number on the locked door. Shortly after calling, a woman came to unlock the door carrying an armload of eggs, ham, bread, and other dinner items. I shared a dinner table with pilgrims from Korea, Germany, Argentina, Japan, and a man and his dog from Italy who had started his pilgrimage from Rome. Most of them left Saint Jean Pied de Port, France before Christmas. It's interesting that no one at dinner asked why we were walking in winter. The evening was as lively and upbeat as it was during the dinner gatherings in October. The difference was there was little heat in the restaurant and we were all wearing our winter coats.

Lessons learned today: Make sure the phone is connected to a network before relying on it for navigation. It's not always a good idea to walk in the grass on the side of the road to avoid mud; the grass is not packed down and can be muddier.

January 6, 2018 • Day 2 (16)
Hontanas to Población de Campos

Yesterday the Camino broke me in. Today it broke me. I have two friends to share the Camino, Jun from Korea and Maurizio from Italy. During breakfast someone said the weather report predicted snow and freezing temperatures that day. It was snowing when we departed the albergue and it turned to rain after lunch. This created a muddy walk across the Meseta. We walked over the mountain pass of Mostelares as the visibility dropped and the snow hit us from the side. The Meseta messed up my perception of time and distance since it was flat and there was nothing to see on the horizon. I did not seem to be getting anywhere as I walked. On a country road, a Volkswagen pulled over and a man held a basket out of the window. He made a gesture to stamp our pilgrim's passport. It was too cold for him to get out of the car so I handed him my passport and tossed a euro in his basket.

◀ Walking down the mountain pass of Mostelares. The snow was blowing sideways from the right.

Castrojeriz ▶

The three of us stopped for lunch in a small village and I was surprised how inexpensive the food and drinks cost. A sandwich and café latte was 2.5 euros. Back home the latte alone would have been $3.50. After a tough day of walking we finally arrived at the albergue as it turned dark outside. We had left Hontanas at 8:30 a.m. and arrived at 6:30 p.m. Dinner in the albergue was fantastic. We had more wine than we could drink and two more pilgrims from Korea and Spain joined us for dinner.

Lessons learned today: Use caution when removing headphones from your pocket. The rubber earpiece fell off and I had to walk back 50 feet to look for it. It fell in an area covered with fragments of manure, which resembled the earbud. Also, keep candy bars somewhere in the pack where they won't freeze. I nearly broke a tooth biting into a frozen Snickers bar.

January 7, 2018 • Day 3 (17)
Población de Campos to Calzadilla de la Cueza

It was nice walking without rain or mud today. The temperatures were also above freezing. The Korean pilgrim, Jun, woke up sick after the difficult walk yesterday. He told Maurizio and I to leave the albergue without him. We trekked along a narrow dirt road through a vast farmland. The long, straight road seemed to go on forever. We entered the town of Carrión de los Condes and began getting passed by people running in the street. We rounded a corner near the town square and accidentally entered the area roped off for the finish line of a town marathon. The cheering spectators lined the street. They looked disappointed and began frowning at us. A gentleman, who appeared to be a race official, was holding up the perimeter rope, we needed little translation. As we ducked under the rope, I caught my backpack momentarily sending me in a stumble. But we safely made our way past the crowd without hooking a spectator's wardrobe with our trekking poles. I was hoping that we wouldn't show up on Spanish social media for slowing down the runners.

◀ Arriving at the albergue

We arrived at the albergue earlier in the day, which gave us time to do laundry. Four of us split the cost by combining our clothes. There was a generous amount of food for dinner and more wine than we could drink. After dinner I assisted Maurizio by calling albergues 30 to 50 kilometers ahead to plan lodging for the next day. A challenge of walking in January is that few albergues remain open, and fewer still willing to accommodate Maurizio's Alaskan husky malamute.

LESSONS LEARNED TODAY: Start the day's walk with a faster pace to avoid arriving in the dark. Periodically check backpack hip-belt for tightness. The shoulder straps started taking the weight and my upper body started to hurt. The hips should have all the weight of the backpack.

A small church ▶ and picnic area in the middle of a vast farmland along the Camino.

January 8, 2018 • Day 4 (18)
Calzadilla de la Cueza to El Burgo Ranero

The temperature was -3 °C when we started out in the morning darkness. Maurizio fell on a patch of ice during the walk out of town. I looked to see if his husky malamute would pull him across the ice. Today was the best weather day with blue skies. Our group separated early as each of us found a different speed to walk. Maurizio was by far in the best shape and disappeared ahead of me. I walked solo for 9 hours. We communicated on WhatsApp and met up in Sahagún for lunch. We would meet again at the albergue at the end of the day. The Koreans did not walk as far, so we did not see them again.

In El Burgo Ranero we joined at dinner four other pilgrims who had left Saint Jean Pied de Port on the 20th of December. Dinner wasn't provided in the albergue so Maurizio volunteered to cook an Italian meal.

I had started the Camino in the Province of Burgos and then crossed into the Province of Palencia. Today I crossed into the Province of León. This would be similar to crossing states in the U.S.

Lessons learned today: Bring a longer charging cord for the phone to be able to type emails when the phone is charging. I brought a headlamp to use, due to the shorter daylight hours, and I should start using it to avoid slipping on ice in the morning. I shouldn't rest too long throughout the day because it becomes incredibly difficult to start moving again.

Crossing the bridge over rio Esla in Mansilla de Las Mulas

January 9, 2018 • Day 5 (19)
Burgo Ranero to León

Again the temperature today was -3 °C and it began snowing an hour into the walk. I wasn't planning to walk more than 32 kilometers each day like my Italian friend Maurizio. However, it's made the walk so much more enjoyable trekking with at least one other person. If I finish early I might continue walking to the ocean. Time will tell. Many pilgrims are walking in winter for the same reasons: less busy work schedules, no crowds, and cooler temperatures. In the summer months, walking in high heat can be dangerous. I am well-prepared for low temps and snow, but the relentless cold rain has been another matter. Today I welcomed the snow because it cushioned each step along the walk. My feet have been swelling during the walk and in León I replaced my trail runners.

LESSONS LEARNED TODAY: When you cinch down on the rain jacket hood, make sure you're not pulling the cord to your headphones. I pulled my headphones out and had to look for my earbud in the snow. When purchasing a pair of hiking boots/trail runners buy a larger size to accommodate foot swelling.

Sidewalk in Mansilla de Las Mulas ▶

January 10, 2018 • Day 6 (20)
Astorga to Foncebadón

Today I leapfrogged to Astorga since my brother and I walked this stage in 2016. Foncebadón is 2,025 feet higher than Astorga and it started to snow early in the day as I gained elevation. I reached the Monte Irago albergue in whiteout conditions. During dinner I overheard a pilgrim say the blizzard will last 4 days and make walking impossible in the morning.

◀ The road is beginning to be covered with snow. Within a few hours the road was closed to cars.

◀ The cross at Foncebadón.

The trees did very little ▶
to block the falling snow.
The handkerchief froze
below my chin.

Approaching Cruz de Ferro—
The mound around the cross
are stones "burdens" left by
pilgrims over the years

January 11, 2018 • Day 7 (21)
Foncebadón to Ponferrada

Today was the most challenging day on the Camino as I ascended the remaining elevation to Cruz de Ferro in the blowing snow. It was still dark when I departed the albergue. Walking on the road was my only option because the snow was over a foot deep on the trail. There is a tradition that pilgrims bring a stone from their homeland to leave behind at Cruz de Ferro. This symbolizes leaving behind burdens in life. The road started to thaw out at the bottom of the mountain. I passed through El Acebo, which looked like a village in the movie Lord of the Rings. At the base of the mountain I had lunch in Molinaseca where I crossed a bridge built by the Romans. In Ponferrada I had my pilgrim's passport stamped inside the Castle of the Knights Templar, which was built in the 12th century. I checked into a hotel since I needed good sleep. There is always someone snoring in the albergues and earplugs only help so much. I'll stay an extra day in Ponferrada to rest my body. It will also give me a chance to explore the city.

Leaving my burdens behind ▶

January 12, 2018 • Rest day
Rest day Ponferrada

I enjoyed a day to explore Ponferrada. I visited an outfitter store to buy better equipment for the winter weather. I purchased hiking boots because the trail runners I replaced in León had little ankle support and I felt my ankle collapsing on the walk from El Acebo. This makes the third pair of North Face footwear on the Camino. Now I know where all the shoes come from that are littering the Camino. I left mine in the albergue offering them to the next pilgrim. I also purchased a better hat and waterproof covers to go over my fleece gloves. I was the only person touring the Castillo de los Templarios and the Basílica de Nuestra Señora de La Encina, another reminder of low tourism in January. It was fun to use the Google translator app to decipher the various historical information signs in the fortress. I met up with Maurizio for dinner, and he told me a harrowing story of his trek to Foncebadón in whiteout conditions. His husky malamute didn't seem to mind the snow, however.

◀ Molinaseca

Knights Templar Castle ▶

January 13, 2018 • Day 8 (22)
Ponferrada to Villafranca del Bierzo

The walk to Villafranca was easy today with light rain and snow. All the water fountains were frozen shut during this stage. I filled my water reservoir from a broken spigot that froze during the night. My Camino app calls the next day's stage, "the mother of all stages." I stopped for breakfast outside of Ponferrada and enjoyed a conversation with the owner of the restaurant. I mentioned that I planned to walk to O Cebreiro the next day and he discouraged me and suggested I take the alternative route around. He said, "my father lives near O Cebreiro and he told me the snow was too deep to drive." From behind the bar he opened the internet on his computer to the webcam in O Cebreiro and showed me a picture of the amount of snow in the town. The conditions looked bad. I took a picture of the webcam image with my phone. My brother had called this climb "a real ass-kicker." At this point on the Camino I met very few pilgrims.

◀ Frozen vineyard

Broken spigot at a ▶
frozen water fountain

January 14, 2018 • Day 9 (23)
Villafranca del Bierzo to Hospital de la Condesa

The day's hike was very strenuous. My brother wasn't lying when he said this stage was an ass-kicker. When I crossed into the Province of Galicia I would start seeing changes in culture, language and even the shape of the houses. As I entered the village of O Cebreiro I was passed by a vehicle carrying backpacks from the pilgrims in the albergue. I decided not to stay in O Cebreiro because I wanted to finish the gain in elevation so I could start downhill tomorrow. I was the only pilgrim in the albergue at Hospital de la Condesa.

◀ Muddy areas on the climb to O Cebreiro

Marker entering the ▶
Province of Galicia

January 15, 2018 • Day 10 (24)
Hospital de la Condesa to Sarria

I passed the physical stage with the mountains now behind me. The Galician trails were overgrown with ferns, and the trees draped by overgrown moss. It's the first time seeing an abundance of streams. I do not have to worry about ice on the trail any longer because the temperatures are above freezing. A dog nipped at the draw cord on my gaiters today and I had to place my trekking pole between my legs and his teeth until I was far from the village. At another village a small mutt followed me through the streets until he noticed several other larger dogs, then he turned to me and started barking. He may have started barking to show the other dogs he wasn't with me. I received a WhatsApp message from Maurizio informing me that the Korean group I had been walking with last week had taken a bus from Astorga to O Cebreiro, bypassing the hardest part of the Camino.

◀ I left the main road trudging through more snow, and as a 14th century church appears my MP3 player started playing "Hallelujah"

The snow is finally behind me

January 16, 2018 • Day 11 (25)
Sarria to Gonzar

I stopped for lunch in Moimentos where the bar owner asked me if others were coming. I assured him that I had passed 13 pilgrims. He seemed anxious to have business during the low season. I passed the town of Portomarín which was built next to a Roman bridge over the Minho (Miño) River. In the 1960s the Minho River was dammed to create the Belesar reservoir, putting the old village of Portomarín under water. Because the water level was low, remains of ancient buildings, and the old bridge, are visible today. Before arriving in Gonzar I walked through a forest that was devastated by a previous fire. I was the only one staying at the municipal albergue in Gonzar.

◀ The landscapes changed at virtually every turn

Roman bridge at ▶
Portomarín

January 17, 2018 • Day 12 (26)
Gonzar to Melide

A short walk from the albergue I detoured to explore the excavation site of an ancient pre-Roman settlement called Castro de Castromaior. This is one of the most important archaeological sites of the Iron Age in the Iberian Peninsula. Later in the morning I passed "Crucero" cross of Lameiros, which dates back to 1670. In the town of Furelos, I walked over a medieval bridge built in the 12th century. I was struck by all the vandalism on the concrete Camino distance markers along the way. It's sad to also see the brass mileage placards stolen, and tiles depicting the scallop shells missing. I only started seeing the vandalism within 100 km of Santiago. Today I started to feel each step bringing me closer to the end of the Camino. I haven't decided whether to use the extra two days to walk to the coast, which is the distance between Albuquerque and Santa Fe, New Mexico. Tomorrow I plan to walk to O Pedrouzo (O Pino), which includes 20 miles of walking up and down hills.

◀ Pre-Roman settlement called Castro de Castromaior

Medieval bridge at Furelos ▶

January 18, 2018 • Day 13 (27)
Melide to Santiago de Compostela

I decided not to stop in O Pedrouzo today, but rather push my endurance, arriving at Santiago de Compostela after walking over 32 miles (53 km) in 12.5 hours. I was inspired to keep walking by the enchanting landscapes along the route. Combining all the hill elevations, I walked down 4,287 feet and walked up 3,582 feet. There were three cows waiting for me to pass before following me. I walked faster to lose them, no bull! I did not need a lot of food to sustain my energy level today. I ate a croissant and a banana this morning. Stopped for a light lunch at noon and ate some snack mix toward the end of the day. I walked 3 days ahead of schedule and decided to not walk to the ocean. I met the objectives and accomplished my goal. Walking to the ocean may be a reason to return someday.

◀ This forest reminded me of Hansel and Gretel.

Three cows following me ▶

January 19, 2018
Santiago de Compostela

Other pilgrims started arriving Santiago later in the day and it was amazing to watch the new arrivals in the cathedral square. To see the joy and tears on their faces was very moving. A Spaniard I had lunch with is a regular celebrity who has been in Spanish news having completed the Camino 28 times from various starting points. I'll stay another day in Santiago at the historic Hotel Parador Santiago de Compostela and meet up with Maurizio and Nanook when they arrive in Santiago tomorrow.

◀ Entrance to a dark logging forest

Santiago de ▶ Compostela on the day following my arrival

Going up the mountain before reaching Cruz de Ferro and after losing the dog in Foncebadon

Interview with a Winter Pilgrim

Linnea Hendrickson, who has walked several Caminos, and who loves to read Camino accounts, had asked to interview me about my winter pilgrimage. She had followed my Facebook posts and scheduled my presentation to the local chapter of American Pilgrims on the Camino, a non-profit group devoted to "fostering the enduring tradition of the Camino." She originally thought that the interview might make a short article for La Concha, the association's electronic newsletter. However, before either of us realized what was happening, the interview questions inspired the extended account of my pilgrim journey that has essentially become this book.

Linnea, who has a background in English and children's literature, and who has also done much writing of her own, helped edit my sometimes awkward and unwieldy prose into something much clearer and more enjoyable to read.

The birth of an idea

Why did you decide to walk the Camino?

After seeing the movie "The Way," I received pictures from my brother of his biking adventures in the Chihuahuan dessert at Big Bend, National Park. I suggested he watch the movie, which had scenes of bicyclists on the Camino. Shortly after, he suggested I join him in walking the Camino de Santiago. I did a few Google searches, and wrote back with a yes.

We had not spoken much since our stepfather's passing, and hadn't seen much of each other in recent years. This would be an opportunity to spend extended time together, and also put myself on a spiritual journey.

A CHANGE OF PLANS

Why did you have to leave early? What happened next?

I still feel bad about this. We had been planning our Camino for fifteen months, and I had approval to take the time off from work. But just before arriving in Burgos I received a work email informing me I needed a visa for my next work assignment. We reviewed our plans and realized there was not enough time for me to finish the Camino and we agreed to skip the Meseta and take the "train of shame" from Burgos to León. Then, after two days of walking from León, I received another email informing me I would be needed in Houston right away to start processing for the visa.

The bus station, just a block away from our housing in Astorga, was still open, allowing me to purchase a ticket. My brother continued from Astorga alone.

Note: when you show up at the Madrid airport without a reservation, ask for a round-trip ticket instead of a one-way ticket. The one-way ticket was well over a thousand dollars more expensive. I'm grateful to the attendant for pointing that out to me. I had an inner chuckle when she asked for my return date.

Finishing what I started

Why did you decide to go back to finish the Camino on your own and in January?

The thought of not finishing what I had started did not sit well with me. Arranging the time off from work and coordinating with someone else would be difficult. In early December 2017, I was going through a difficult time with something that was out of my control. I thought, where in the world would I rather be? It dawned on me "Why not head back to Spain and finish the Camino next month?" After a few online searches to check the weather along the route, I realized that walking in winter was a real possibility.

PREPARING

What preparations did you make for your winter Camino?

I didn't want to repeat my mistakes from the first Camino so I started a list of lessons learned. Three discouraging things stood out in my online winter pilgrimage research.

- First, you'll need more gear (and thus more weight)
- Second, many albergues will be closed
- And third, there are fewer hours of daylight in which to walk

I saw no warnings about walking in snow.

I made some assessments based on my list of lessons learned and realized that I would need to add just one extra base layer (thermal underwear) and a slightly heavier jacket. Those items would be worn each day and would not add to my pack weight. Ultimately, my winter pack weight was 18.2 pounds (before water) and far lighter than it was on my first Camino. The pack weight was also in line with the recommended 10% of body weight. On my first Camino, my pack was 26 pounds, and would eventually lead to a knee injury.

I downloaded a Camino pilgrim's app and familiarized myself with it prior to paying the 6.5 euros for the unlocked Camino Frances route. The phone app showed the stages where there was at least one albergue open year-round.

Having fewer daylight hours was not a hindrance. I often walked longer than normal stage because it was still daylight, and I did not want to sit for hours in an albergue waiting for dinner. Some mornings I started walking in the dark, I used my headlamp only three times, one of which was during the evening of the last day. In the morning darkness, icy areas were easy to see in the reflected moonlight. When I walked around a town at night I could still see residual water puddles in the light from the street lamps. I just treated them as ice.

Thus the three negatives turned out to be non-issues.

I decided to walk alone because I wanted to finish the segments I missed in 2016. I am also used to hiking and snowshoeing alone in New Mexico in the months I have off between job rotations. I learned from my reading and from conversations with pilgrims I met, that many people walk the Camino in winter because their jobs keep them busy other times of the year. I remember some anxiety about finding a bed on the first Camino because of the large number of pilgrims pouring into the albergues. My brother and I noticed people sleeping on a basketball court in Villamayor de Monjardín due to the bed shortage. I looked forward to the winter experience of not having to wait for a shower, and having better sleep without dozens of people snoring in cadence.

This time I started in Burgos because my brother and I had leapfrogged to León when we first thought we could finish the Camino by skipping the Meseta (I still feel bad for him having missed it). I walked across the Meseta from Burgos to León and then took a train to Astorga, since I had already walked that stage in 2016. From Astorga I continued along the Camino Frances through Foncebadón, Ponferrada, Villafranca de Bierzo, Hospital de la Condesa, Sarria, Gonzar, and Melide. I turned right instead of left at Triacastela, not walking through Samos, a route I found shorter and more remote.

Busy season vs winter

What was the difference between walking with your brother in a busier season and walking alone in the winter?

Aside from not having a sounding board or a social source of sympathy during some of the hardships on the Camino, by walking alone I didn't feel any pressure to keep up with someone when I stopped to take pictures. I told my brother early on to keep walking when I would stop to take pictures, but I expended a lot of energy walking twice as fast to catch up. One of the biggest differences was that

Walking in 2016 with David.

2016 walking past crowds approaching Astorga

the evenings in October were more social during dinnertime. There were more casual conversations in the albergues, because there were far more English-speaking people walking the Camino in the fall. Something I learned about myself walking in winter was that when I have my alone time I get charged up and seem to have all the energy in the world. On my first trip I remember feeling completely drained of energy each morning when my brother and I stayed in crowded albergues. The large masses of pilgrims in October seem to draw the energy right out of me. I had the exact opposite experience in the winter, which directly contributed to my ability to walk abnormally long distances each day.

January challenges
What were the biggest challenges you faced while walking alone in January?

When my feet started swelling they would hurt. The North Face trail runners I wore at the beginning were not large enough to accommodate my feet swelling during the walk. I had a lot of pain in the mornings when I first put on my shoes and began walking. The pain in my left foot continued for weeks after the Camino and my left foot's small toe is still red. I was unable to replace my shoes until León, by then I had already walked 5 days.

At a mall in León I struggled to find the size I needed in a waterproof hiking shoe. The one I settled for was only a half size larger and I would later find out that it did not provide enough ankle support. It would be two more days of walking and feeling my feet collapse periodically on the rocky trails before I could buy another pair. In Ponferrada I found an outfitter store where I was able to purchase a proper hiking boot.

If it wasn't raining, it was snowing and my fleece gloves became saturated. One day I had to remove the gloves because they were so wet. I kept my hands in my jacket to keep them warm, which didn't allow me to use the trekking poles. Among my purchases in Ponferrada were thin, light-weight,

A steep snowy climb before arriving in O Cebreiro

water and wind proof mittens that went over my fleece gloves. I also bought a proper winter hat with a retractable face cover.

The most disappointing choice of gear I brought turned out to be my goose down jacket. The puffy down jackets are popular these days. They are ultra lightweight and warm while you're standing still. However, when you walk for hours on end, these jackets become so saturated in sweat that they feel soggy. The ultra lightweight down sleeping bag was great to sleep in, but the jacket was a disaster. I was able to buy a polyester hoodie in León, allowing me to exchange the wet down jacket for the hoodie. The hoodie was also a nice lightweight layer to use with my rain jacket.

There were many days when the temperatures were below freezing and while wearing all layers I still felt cold. My merino wool base layer was too thin. I will evaluate the compromise between weight, wicking, and warmth in a mid-layer jacket for future treks. It didn't take me long to realize that I had to constantly adjust my layers of clothing while walking. During portions of the steep climb to O Cebreiro there were freezing winds, and snow, but I removed my jacket and hoodie and wore only a merino wool base and a rain jacket. Despite the cold I overheated from sheer physical exertion, and also needed to dry out from sweating.

Albergues in Winter

You said most municipal albergues were open during the winter. Were many people staying in them with you?

I was alone in a municipal albergue called Xunta de Galicia in the village of Hospital de la Condesa, west of O Cebreiro. I was also alone in the municipal albergue in Gonzar. In Sarria there was only one other pilgrim and only two others in the municipal albergue in Burgos. In Foncebadón the albergue was nearly full and the municipal albergue in Hontanas had all the lower bunk beds taken. Villafranca del Bierzo had 20 people, and all the other albergues had anywhere from 5 to 10 people staying the night. I stayed in hotels in Ponferrada and Melide, which provided a nice break.

Albergue in Calzadilla de la Cueza

Warm Water

Did you have heat? Hot showers?

They don't all turn the heat on! In the municipal albergue in Hontanas the hospitalera poured a bag of pellets into a pellet stove while everyone was getting ready for bed. I was thankful that someone poured another bag in the stove some time before we all woke up. There was no heat in the municipal albergue in El Burgo Ranero. A Korean pilgrim fed logs into a wood burning stove downstairs until the late evening hours. I have to admit; it felt not much warmer sleeping upstairs than outside. When I woke up in the morning I noticed the same Korean man was still feeding the stove. I'm not sure if he stayed up all night or if he woke up early to start a fire. The other albergues had some form of heat but the temperature varied. All albergues had warm showers. However, some took longer than others to warm up.

Feelings and Fears

How did it feel walking in the snow? Did you ever fear for your safety or get lost?

I absolutely loved walking in the snow and my feet stayed warm the entire Camino. While walking in snow my feet no longer felt sharp rocks and loose stones. I had no anxiety about my safety. The only time I was nervous was when I heard several gunshots just outside a small town in a mountainous area. It was local hunters shooting game but I could not see them and didn't know which way they were shooting. With a Camino phone app it's difficult to get lost. Without the app I can see how easy it would be when the fog moves in.

I will admit that on two occasions I was distracted by my MP3 player, lost in thought, when I missed a turn. A logging truck came out of nowhere and stopped behind me. I wondered why it was waiting on the road. I stopped walking and looked down at my cell phone. Then the truck resumed its travel down the road. My app showed I had walked a full kilometer down the wrong road. The truck driver was probably going to inform me that I was going in the wrong direction. I remember taking a short cut through the forest to re-intersect the trail and found the Camino running below a steep embankment. I ultimately had to walk back up a hill to find a less steep way to get down. My first day in Burgos a nice lady pulled her car over to the side of the road to inform me I was walking the wrong direction, since my phone had yet to connect to the cell network it led me in the wrong direction.

CHALLENGING SECTIONS
Which were the most challenging sections of the Camino?

By far the most challenging section was before reaching Foncebadón in whiteout conditions. I departed Astorga and began a gradual uphill walk. It began to rain a few hours later and as I gained elevation the rain turned to snow. The snow on the trail became deeper than I had seen before, and it was getting difficult to walk. Since the trail paralleled the main road I decided to walk on the road instead, since some tire tracks were still visible. I hadn't seen any cars for a while and I figured if I heard a car coming I would make my way to the side of the road. I took a short video clip that shows just how much the wind was blowing and snowing sideways during that walk. It was painful to remove my gloves to switch my phone to video because it was below freezing.

I entered Foncebadón without my glasses on because they were too fogged to see through. I was also trying to pull my hood down to shield my face from the weather and my glasses were in the way. I had to stop periodically, stick my trekking poles in the snow so they would stand on end, and remove my glove again to access the map on my pilgrim's app in order to see where I was in relation to the

Foncebadón–
Ponferrada —
Footprints in
the snow

albergue. By the time I entered the small village of Foncebadón the snow was almost a half-foot deep and I felt my trekking pole drop through a grate in the middle of the road. As I was pulling to remove it I could hear a car behind me spinning tires. I turned around and I was only a foot away from a bumper where someone noticed me at the last minute and hit the brakes. The car ended up getting stuck in the snow when it came to a stop. I removed my trekking pole and made my way to the albergue. I was lucky the car did not plow into me.

The next morning it was still dark outside and the snow continued to blow. The few pilgrims who were up at 7:00 a.m. and downstairs having cereal were discussing the weather forecast. Someone mentioned the weather would be bad for the next few days and the snow would only get deeper. By the time I had a cup of coffee, a bowl of cereal and some bread I began donning all my jackets, raincoat and gaiters. I was ready to don my pack when more pilgrims came downstairs and started taking turns opening the front door to film video of the blowing snow outside with their phones. I also took a video clip.

◀ Snow out the window at the Foncebadón albergue. (inset)

As I put on my pack, the other pilgrims looked at me as if I was crazy to set out in the darkness in blowing snow. I wished everyone farewell and told them that I wasn't going to be stuck in the albergue for the next two days roasting chestnuts over the fire. I tried to walk up the main street in Foncebadón but the snow was at least a foot deep and I was already feeling fatigued about 100 feet from the albergue. A dog followed me up the street and seemed to be unaffected by the depth of the snow, he just cheerfully hopped along. I looked at my pilgrim's app and noticed the main road intersected the Camino trail at the top of the mountain before Cruz de Ferro, so I turned around to head back toward the main road.

The snow on the main road was only 6 to 8 inches deep but there were no car tracks to walk in. The road was closed. As I made my way up the road the dog ran past me. I yelled at him to go back but he wouldn't leave. I thought to myself that maybe I needed to say something in Spanish, but didn't know the translation. I continued hoping he would return home. Further from the village I found a van stuck on the side of the road that must have belonged to the folks who arrived at the albergue late in the evening. I stopped to see if someone was inside, then turned to see someone following me up the road. It was the owner of the van coming back to retrieve something from inside.

"Is this your dog?" I asked him. He said "no." I told him I did not want the dog to follow me to Cruz de Ferro. He said the dog was a stray and he would walk with me to the next town. "No," I said. "The dog will die in the weather." He reluctantly agreed to hold onto his collar until I made my way up the road. At this point I was trying to walk faster to distance myself from the dog. With the dog now behind me, I stopped to rest at a Camino road sign figuring it was a good place to take a selfie to show the weather conditions. It was this selfie that I shared with friends and family back home showing my glasses fogged, and the cotton handkerchief that was blocking the snow on my face frozen solid beneath my chin.

Cruz de Ferro finally appeared on the horizon as the wind started to subside. I turned to take a picture behind me to show the only tracks in the snow leading up the mountain. Not to sound selfish but it was special having Cruz de Ferro all to myself. I removed the stone from my homeland, that represented burdens to leave behind, and left it in a small impression atop this enormous snow covered mound. Saying a prayer for a snowplow did not occur to me.

I looked for the Camino trail at Cruz de Ferro but didn't find it. It appeared to blend into the winter landscape so the road was my only option. There was less strain on my legs walking downhill, but I kept hoping a vehicle or snowplow would come along before I reached the bottom of the mountain. Halfway down the mountain I heard an engine revving. As I made my way to the side of the road I saw a land cruiser approaching. As the vehicle passed I saw the occupants inside looking at me through the window with surprised expressions on their faces. They waved at me as their vehicle with four tire chains cut two tire tracks into the deep snow. "Thank you so much." I said, realizing that it was impossible for them to hear me. I followed the narrow tire track placing each foot carefully in front of me trying not to lose balance in the snow. A snowplow finally passed just as I was arriving in El Acebo, but the remaining walk down the mountain remained challenging while I had to avoid falling on the road where ice had begun to form.

◀ Cruz de Ferro

Memorable encounters

What were some of your more memorable encounters with people along the way?

I met Spaniards, men from Japan, Brazil, Germany, and a woman from Argentina. I lost count of how many Korean men and women I met. Using "Google Translate" I communicated with a Korean and learned he was retired, and owned a sailboat. He showed me the pictures on his phone, and told me how he found true love in his homeland. I mostly trekked with Maurizio and his husky malamute, Nanook, who began their Camino from Rome. They went on to complete the Camino after three months of walking. A short walk from Hontanas, Maurizio took Nanook off his leash to let him explore the trail ahead of us. He shouted commands, "come back Nanook, stay off the road, no Nanook, Nanook, no Nanook." But the dog didn't obey. "Don't you need to ask him in Italian?" I asked him. He then shouted commands in Italian and the dog turned and started running back to us. Rather than using the dog's native language he was using English for my benefit. Maurizio kept a faster pace than me so we agreed on which albergue to meet at the end of the day.

◀ Walking the Meseta in mud with Italian and Korean

Camino Angels

People often meet "angels" on the Camino. Were there any moments when you felt you encountered "angels"?

There were no trail angels, other than the woman who pulled her car over in Burgos and told me I was walking in the wrong direction and the logging truck driver who stopped and waited until I turned around after seeing me walking in the wrong direction. On the path near Calzada del Coto, where the Camino splits in two directions, there was a Spaniard at the crossroad hesitant which way to walk. I assisted him with the Camino app on my phone by showing him how much further he would walk taking the path to the right. A path that runs along the ancient Roman Way (one of the best preserved stretches, as per the app). Since I would be meeting with my Italian friend in El Burgo Ranero, I took the shorter path to the left. The Spaniard was grateful that I saved him kilometers of extra walking and he decided to follow me. I hope someone enjoys the Roman road.

Walking to O Cebreiro

Tell us about walking to O Cebreiro, alone in the snow, after people cautioned you to take the road. What was it like when you reached the top?

At the Ave Fénix Pilgrims Hostel in Villafranca del Bierzo I met my first Americans during dinner. They were four university students from South Carolina in their early twenties on winter break. I shared that dinner table with more than 20 others from various countries. During dinner I overheard discussions about using baggage-forwarding service for the walk to O Cebreiro. People also discussed going the alternative route along one of the less busy roads because the depth of snow was reported to be too deep on the trail. I showed the

Photograph of webcam in O Cebreiro ▶

O Cebreiro webcam picture on my phone to three Koreans sitting across the table from me. They looked up from the picture with surprised looks, looking to me for words of advice. "Are you going the alternative route?" One asked me. "No." I said. "I have planned to walk in snow from the beginning of my Camino." I explained. The next morning while walkers were still shuffling into the dining room to eat, I was already fastening my gaiters and getting ready to head out. There were familiar stares from the others, stares that implied, "What's your rush?"

After departing alone from the albergue I met only a few people stirring in Villafranca de Bierzo. It

A quick stop at the Galicia marker

A sign the road ahead may be a challenge

was quiet and cold. The town reminded me of Astoria, Oregon in the way the houses were built on the hillside. From Villafranca the ascent began gradually but would grow steeper until it became, "impracticable," [sic] The phone app also referred to this section as, "The mother of all stages!" I was mentally preparing myself for this crazy incline, but the elevation was just a steady uphill walk. On the back of a road sign someone had spray painted an advertisement to rent a horse to O Cebreiro. This was my first indication that the elevation ahead was a challenge. Why else would someone want to rent a horse? At a small village near the base of the mountain the elevation was suppose to get steeper, so I had lunch before going further. After lunch it started snowing and soon I was walking in snow and mud. Halfway up, the wind and snow increased.

I had to remind myself that as cold, windy and exhausted I was from the climb; I should stop to look around at the incredible views of the mountain and valleys below. At the monument where the trail crossed into the province of Galicia, I stopped to rest and take pictures of the scenery. When I stopped hiking to look at the views, my body temperatures dropped and I had to remove my pack to add layers of clothing. When I finally arrived at the town of O Cebreiro, it was crowded with people and kids of all ages sledding down hillsides.

Two Koreans were looking for the albergue among the buildings. The three of us had to be careful not to be run over by passing cars. While I was talking with the Korean couple, a vehicle started honking as it was pulling off the road. I recognized the driver from the Ave Fenix Pilgrims Hostel, who was waving his hand at me through the window. He looked happy to see I had made it to the top of the mountain. In the back of his Land Rover I could see the bags he was transporting for the other pilgrims, piled to the ceiling inside. The three of us entered a restaurant to ask for directions to the O Cebreiro albergue. The restaurant was crowded. Every table and barstool was full, and with people waiting near the entrance to be seated. Because it was too busy to get the staff's attention, we exited without directions.

Land Rover piled high with packs from Ave Fenix Pilgrims Hostel

Once outside I opened the map on my phone and showed the Korean couple that the albergue was not far from where we were standing. "I don't want to stay here tonight. There are too many people. I will keep walking while I still have daylight."

"I'm tired." The woman said, looking at her husband. We bade each other farewell, "Buen Camino" and I headed to the main road and started walking out of town.

The phone app showed a hotel in the next town. It also showed that the albergue next to the hotel was closed for the winter. By the time O Cebreiro disappeared behind me the sun was getting low on the horizon. I arrived at Linares, and as in

O Cebreiro, there were dozens of cars parked all over the small village, with kids running their sleds up and down hillsides. The Casa Jaime hotel bar was packed with people and it was difficult to find someone to ask about a room. A woman asked me a question in Spanish but I did not understand. "Do you have a room?" I asked, trying to listen to her over the loud voices and music playing in the bar. "No rooms. Two kilometers." She said in English. This was the first time on the Camino that anxiety set in. I would be sleeping in the snow if I didn't find lodging. Out in the parking lot I searched my phone app for another albergue two kilometers from my position. I was certainly not going to retrace my steps to O Cebreiro in the dark.

The pilgrim's app showed that the next albergue was Xunta de Galicia Pilgrims Hostel in the small village of Hospital del la Condesa, a municipal albergue that should be open year round. Most importantly there was a phone number. In the setting sun, I called the number. A lady answered who did not speak English. I tried to ask her if the albergue was open with a combination of Spanish and English. "Peregrino, esta noche, open?" I said to her. "Open sí." She said. "Excelente, mucho gracias, I come now." I said. Hoping she would understand the last part. "Sí." She repeated over the phone before we hung up. I was cold and exhausted but confident the woman I spoke with understood my intention to arrive that evening. During the walk from Linares I began contemplating having to sleep in a barn somewhere if the number I dialed was the wrong albergue a hundred miles away. It took another hour and 1.5 miles (2.4 km) before I arrived at Hospital del la Condesa.

The small snow-covered village was situated on a single street near the main road. It looked frozen in time. There were no people or animals outside in the cold. The village looked abandoned. There was no restaurant or grocery store among the buildings, which left me wondering uneasily whether I had enough snacks in my bag to tide me over until the following day. I was carrying a package of trail mix, two bananas and a package of chocolate donuts. Not the best nutrition for dinner considering how much I had walked that day. But it would have to do for dinner that evening. The sun had finally disappeared below the horizon, and it was starting to get dark. The door to the albergue was unlocked so I let myself in. It was quiet and cold inside. I walked around the two-story building and didn't find any other pilgrims staying there. The shower had hot water and there was one heater turned on downstairs. I had propped up chairs near the heater to start drying my jacket, gloves and raincoat when I heard the front door open.

A woman entered the albergue and stood in the hallway looking at me. She was probably in her 70's. She asked me something in Spanish that I didn't understand. "Hola!" I said, hoping for small talk. She approached me with a look of anger and repeated something in Spanish. I did not understand. "No entiendo." I said to her. Standing a foot away from me now, she then raised her voice and spoke each word slowly. I thought to myself, "Louder and slower will not help me understand." I stood in the hallway cold, hungry and dumb until she finally gave up trying to communicate with me and left. It didn't occur to me to use the Google Translator app on my phone. It would have helped to understand what had upset her.

Shortly thereafter, a younger woman arrived. She greeted me, then turned her attention to opening the small office door in the foyer and started switching breakers behind a panel on the wall. This was the woman I had spoken with on the phone. After she inspected the second story she came downstairs where I was huddled by the only working heater. She invited me to the office where she collected my 6 euros, stamped my pilgrim's passport, and handed me a municipal albergue receipt granting permission to sleep that night. I followed her upstairs where she walked around the bunk beds ensuring all the heaters were working.

Then she turned to me and said, "Buen Camino." As she made her way downstairs I heard the front door locking behind her. "I guess it's just me tonight," I thought to myself.

I could not believe how quiet the albergue was. The upstairs was packed full of bunk beds, so I chose the one nearest the heater. Before falling asleep I calculated the miles and the difficulty of the day's walk. I realized that by walking from Villafranca del Bierzo to Hospital del la Condesa, considering the elevation gained, it would have been similarly compared to walking from downtown Albuquerque, New Mexico to the parking lot at the base of the Sandia Mountains, walking up the La Luz trail and half way down the back side of the mountain. I had walked 22.46 miles (36 km) almost entirely uphill that day. The Fitbit showed I burned 4,730 calories and there would only be the snacks to eat that evening. Knowing the other pilgrims were back in O Cebreiro finishing up a festive dinner together, it made me consider if I made the right decision to keep walking. But there was something special about having the albergue to myself. The quiet alone time was a much-needed moment to recharge my mind and body after the long uphill walk. I would be half way through the next stage when I started walking the next morning. I would sleep alone in one more municipal albergue in Gonzar before arriving in Melide.

The last push

What changed after Sarria? What made you decide to walk the last 53 km from Melide all the way to Santiago in one day?

In Sarria I stayed at Albergue Credencial, which was very modern and had 28 plus beds and a restaurant. There was only one other pilgrim, from Spain, staying in the albergue, and he snored all night, a reminder to wear earplugs no matter how few people are staying in the albergue.

I counted 13 pilgrims on the walk from Sarria to Melide. This was the most I had seen in a day on this winter Camino. I passed most of them shortly after I began walking due to the pace I was keeping by then. The very low number of pilgrims who started walking from Sarria is a reminder that the majority of pilgrims avoid the Camino in winter. According to the "Camino Ways" website 278,232 pilgrims completed the Camino de Santiago in 2016, a figure based on the total number of Compostelas issued by the cathedral in Santiago, a total of 176,332 had walked the Camino Frances (the route I was walking) in 2016. Although the number of pilgrims on the Camino Frances will vary significantly each day throughout the year, the month of August is the busiest with nearly 55,000 completing the journey in that month.

Graffiti covered 100 KM marker to Santiago de Compostela.

Another online statistic lists 301,036 completing the Camino in 2017 and the trends are showing an increase in numbers each year. Sarria is the most popular starting point for many people to begin their pilgrimage since it meets the minimum 100 kilometers distance for obtaining a Compostela from the cathedral in Santiago.

In Melide I was given a winter discount at the Hotel Restaurante Xaneiro. Many hotels along the Camino offer discounts in winter. Staying in a hotel periodically was a decision I made to ensure there were nights I was properly rested. The Hotel Novo in Ponferrada was only 24 euros, but more than twice as much as an albergue. Since I had walked several stages ahead of schedule the cost wasn't so much a factor in my decision to stay in a hotel. The quality of rest was worth the cost.

That night in Melide I ordered a large pizza for dinner and studied the route between Melide and Santiago on the pilgrim's app. I remember eating the entire pizza with enjoyment. According to the app the elevation gain would be 4,728 feet and the decent would be 3,882 feet, so there would be a tremendous number of hills. The snow was long behind me, and the weather was warming up to between 40° F and 50° F with light rain. In Melide I decided not to stay in another albergue. There is an expression my father said, "A luxury once consumed becomes a necessity." Staying in the hotel with a normal bed and bathtub had spoiled me. I called a few hotels between Melide and Santiago and they were 65 euros or more. I was frustrated because the closer to Santiago the more it cost to stay in a hotel. I made my mind up, if I was too tired, I'd just pay extra and stay at the hotel.

From Melide to Santiago I walked through amazing forests. I came upon a fork in the trail where a cow was waiting for me to pass. After turning left and walking uphill, the cow, and then two others started following me. There was no way I was going to lead these beasts away from their farm, so I picked up the pace and lost them. I was 30 kilometers into my walk when I looked at my pilgrim's app and noticed I had already walked past the town with the hotels. I still had energy to keep going even though the sun was starting to set on the horizon.

I had stopped at a restaurant in a village west of the Santiago airport to fill up my water bladder because I still had miles to walk before reaching Santiago. I ordered several glasses of freshly squeezed orange juice, mesmerized by the way oranges automatically dropped from a rack into the juicer with a push of a button. During this time I was consuming most of the comfort junk food that I had purchased along the way. I could have drank 9 more glasses of orange juice, but by then the sun had fully set and it was dark outside. It was time to go.

A cow waiting for me to pass before following me.

The fall

You fell… that last day—what happened?

I did fall and it was a pretty hard landing. Before I explain how I fell, I have to explain why I was walking backward on a wet street in the dark. During the first stage of the Camino, in 2016, I experienced a lot of knee pain on my walk down the Pyrenees. Having too much weight in my pack was one reason, but it was also the relentless pounding on my knees I experienced walking downhill. There is an alternative route at the top of the Pyrenees that goes to the right and provides for a longer walk but is less steep. My brother and I chose to go straight down. I noticed some people slowly walking backward in the Pyrenees. I tried it, and to my amazement the pain in my knees went away. I decided to integrate walking backwards downhill any time I felt discomfort in my knees, but only if it was safe to do so.

One of the things I like about my backpack is the Stow-on-the-Go trekking pole attachment system, which is designed to quickly attach and carry trekking poles. Sometime after leaving O Cebreiro, during one of my backward walks I started thinking, "What would happen if I fell while my trekking poles were attached to the side of my pack?" I had this image in my mind of falling backwards, snapping the poles, being impaled on one, and dying alone in a forest somewhere on the Camino. I had already thought about what would happen if I choked on an apple slice, and made it a point to be careful while snacking during the walk. Is it morbid to think of the "What ifs?"... I just can't help myself. I am trained from work I go over scenarios to recognize near hits and prevent accidents. So I decided to remove my trekking poles from their stowed position whenever I walked backward down a hill. That way I could throw them away from me if I start to fall.

By the time I reached the outskirts of Santiago I was three days ahead of schedule and I was exhausted. The distance from Melide to Santiago was 53 km and I had already walked for 12 hours. But, I still had to trek across the city to the cathedral. The streets were wet from recent rain, and I was relying on my headlamp to see trip hazards on the ground ahead of me. There is a long downhill stretch prior to crossing a large bridge into the city. Since there were no cars on the road, I decided to walk backward in the street to avoid trip hazards on the sidewalk. While walking backward the strain on my knees eased and the soreness subsided. However, I underestimated the grade of decent in the dark and started building speed.

Distracted by the barking of neighborhood dogs, and preoccupied with switching the song list on my MP3 player. I couldn't bring my foot back fast enough to keep up with my downhill momentum. I fell backward hitting the pavement hard and landing on my trekking poles. My headlamp and MP3 player rolled away from me as my backside came to rest on the pavement. I was laid out in a sprawling mess, as even more dogs barked.

I picked myself up, collected the items in the road, and limped over to the side where I sat on a wall. I put my head in my hands for a moment while my mind raced. Realizing I was lucky to have landed mostly on my backpack, the only noticeable pain was on my left butt cheek. It was a relief to find the trekking poles unbroken after landing on them so hard. I stood up on the sidewalk and assessed my ability to continue. Then I put on my hat and gloves, and began walking again. It would be days later, at home, when I would see the large dark bruise on my butt from falling on my trekking poles.

Before I reached the bridge I saw rows of albergues in the darkness. They looked like army barracks that could accommodate thousands of pilgrims on any given day. I was grateful at that moment to be walking in January, and not in August when tens of thousands descend on Santiago.

Arriving in Santiago

Can you tell us about arriving in Santiago?

I had heard that the first third of the Camino will challenge you physically, the second third will challenge you mentally, and the last third will challenge you emotionally but strengthen you spiritually. Spiritual doesn't necessarily mean a white haired man in the clouds looking down on you. I believe it's a very personal experience and different for everyone.

I was not prepared to be walking through Santiago de Compostela after 8:00 p.m. that night. I was exhausted and worried about the city traffic and getting hit by a car. I decided to leave my headlamp on until I reached the old part of the city. I'm sure it looked weird but I wanted to be as visible as possible. Approaching the old city I stopped seeing arrows and scallop shells and was relying mainly on directions within the pilgrim's app. A man approached me on a narrow street in the old part of the city and pointed me in another direction. I gave a large smile and thanked him. He gave me a smile back and said, "Buen Camino."

I was the only pilgrim walking among the folks, who were out shopping and socializing that evening. I sensed that the cathedral was getting closer because the age and architecture of the buildings changed. By now my legs were completely drained of energy and it took all my effort to keep walking.

As I entered the expansive square in front of the cathedral I experienced overwhelming emotion. There were few people in the square, and an eerie silence surrounded me. I turned around and looked up at the Gothic cathedral, illuminated against the darkness. I felt tears begin to build in my eyes. I could not believe I was there. At that moment I did not feel any pain in my body, I was stunned at the sight before my eyes. After removing my pack and setting it on the ground I continued to stare at the cathedral. I felt a spiritual connection to something far bigger than myself. It was difficult to realize the walk was over.

When I turned to my left and saw the front door to the luxurious Parador Hotel, all the pain in my body came rushing back. I was barely able to pick up my pack and drag myself across the square to the check-in desk.

Interview with a Pilgrim | 87

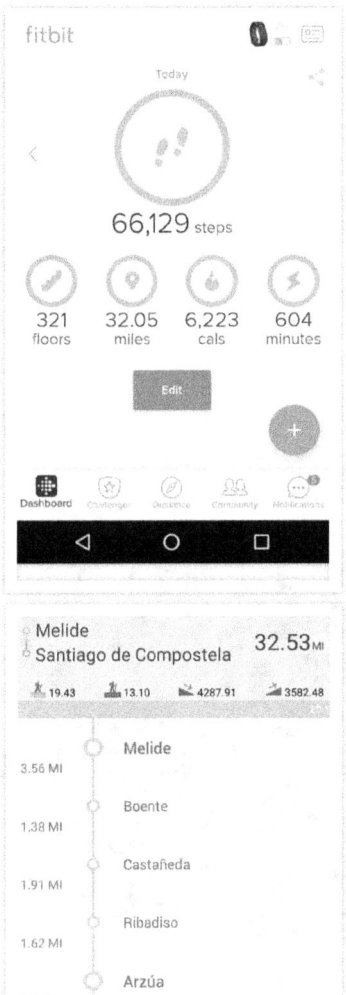

Screen shots of the phone apps tracking my steps from Melide to Santiago de Compostela

WHAT TO PACK

I know you changed some of your gear, at one point. Do you have advice for other winter pilgrims?

You don't need to pack more weight in winter, especially if the gear you have is light-weight. You'll be wearing the additional layers and your pack will essentially be carrying the same items you would have in any other season.

It's hard to place a level of importance on one item over another. Any cold weather hiking requires three layers, and cotton should never be worn. I brought along a cotton handkerchief to use as a sweatband and used it in the higher elevations to cover my face when the blowing snow hit me from the side. The handkerchief did not dry out during the walk and when using it to cover my lower face it froze solid beneath my chin. I bought a polyester face cover in Ponferrada to replace it. A young Spanish couple staying in the albergue in Foncebadón wore cotton jeans. I felt so sorry for them. Their pants were wet and frozen.

The three layers should be a base, amid, and an outer layer (or shell). The base layer I wore each day was a medium weight merino wool shirt and

◀ Wearing the polyester face cover I bought in Ponferrada

long johns. Although my legs and feet stayed warm throughout the Camino, the medium weight was too light and I regretted not buying a heavier one. The mid layer was a goose down jacket, which quickly became my nemesis. If I could start over I would use something other than down.

I chose Marmot® for the rain jacket and pants, but will now consider investing in a Gore-Tex® replacement since the Marmot® was too thin and did not seem to wick moisture away fast enough. Unfortunately it takes a financial investment to get a decent rain jacket that breathes and wicks moisture. A raincoat that does not breathe will make you just as wet from perspiration as the rain would without wearing it, which is why I am not a fan of the non-breathing poncho. My rain pants kept falling down on the walk and required me to frequently pull them up. This was reminder to properly test the gear before leaving home.

The one thing that helped me avoid knee pain was knee support sleeves. Without them I would have not been able to walk the high miles each day without permanent injury. I wore the sleeves for the first two days of the Camino, to allow the surrounding muscles to condition and build strength. I tried removing them for a day, but both knees started to hurt, so they stayed on for the entire Camino. The knee sleeves I purchased from home were heavy and fit my leg too tight. They turned my knees different shades of color and began to irritate my skin. I found the best knee sleeves at a pharmacy on the Camino. They were lightweight, and breathable, with a single lower adjustment strap. After the first Camino in 2016 I had an MRI taken on my left knee due to the pain I was experiencing. I would not have injured myself or felt any discomfort had I been wearing knee sleeves. Also avoid twisting your body and legs when removing your pack at the end of the day. I felt a pop in my left knee while removing my pack in 2016 and it took nearly a year to heal.

I wore silk sock liners on the first Camino and was rewarded with painful blisters. This time I chose to wear toe-sock liners by Injinji®. It took 4 days to get used to the feeling of fabric between my toes but I had no blisters on the winter Camino. I wore a mid weight merino wool sock over the Injinji® socks and my feet were never cold.

I cut my toenails too short on the first Camino and experienced pain from the lack of nail support at the end of the toes. The too-short nail also cut into my skin. If toenails are too long, they will cut holes in the socks; too short, and you're in for pain. A pedicure would be a disaster before you begin the walk because your feet need to be toughened up before starting.

I tried to keep my pack within 10% of my body weight—a rule of thumb for distance hiking. Considering that water is 2.2 pounds or 1 kg per liter, I deliberately put only one liter of water in my reservoir bladder. I kept a lightweight plastic bottle within reach to refill periodically along way. I also used the water bottle to add an electrolyte replacement tablet each day. I only ran out of water once but it was no concern for me because there were so many towns and villages ahead.

Flip-flops allowed me to save pack weight while providing shower shoes and something to wear inside the albergue while my muddy shoes dried out on a shoe rack. The albergue in Villafranca de Bierzo had a shoe rack outside in the cold. If this happens, crumple up a newspaper and shove it into your shoes. This will keep the inside dry during the night.

The flip flops gave me something to wear in the Albergues

The Osprey Stratos 36 backpack was a perfect size, fit and weight, it also came with a rain cover. The pack was small enough to easily fit in the overhead compartment on the airline. The pack had a ridged framework so no matter how my clothing and gear was stuffed inside, it didn't change the way it contoured to my back. I packed all my gear to determine if everything would fit in the pack. The water bladder would not fit inside, even without water in it. My brother suggested suspending the water reservoir on the outside between the mesh backing and the pack. This worked great! It not only freed up more room inside but it also kept the water from freezing since the bladder was directly behind my back. I also added a neoprene sleeve to the reservoir hose to keep it from freezing.

When exchanging dollars to euros, the bank I use back home partners with Deutsche Bank so I did not incur the foreign transaction or ATM fees. It saved me the equivalent cost of two nights stay in an albergue. To avoid using large bills, I withdrew 200 euros from the Deutsche Bank ATM in Madrid. Then I went inside the bank and exchanged the 50 euro notes for 5 euro notes. I decided to use the bank ATM during normal working hours in the unlikely event my debit card might get stuck in the machine. After exchanging the large bills for 5 euro notes I ended up with a thick envelope with 40 notes inside, but it was convenient to pay cash for albergues and food along the way. I had to withdraw more money in Sarria and ultimately paid the fees for using the ATM because the closest

Deutsche Bank was in Madrid. If I could go back and do it again I would have drawn 300 euros and opted for 10 euro notes.

I wouldn't recommend walking the Camino in winter without having a Camino application on your phone. My Verizon iPhone service was $10 per day to add a data plan in Spain. So I purchased an additional unlocked Motorola phone and used T-Mobile, which gave me a less expensive plan in Spain with unlimited data and texting. There was a cell phone signal throughout the Camino, and with unlimited data there were no worries if the albergue had wifi or not.

My Superfeet® insoles were incredible and provided comfort and support for my foot arch. I did not wear the insoles that came with my shoes.

I used several types of earplugs before the Camino to be sure they were comfortable to sleep in and did not fall out during the night. To keep the earplugs from falling out during the night, I kept my ears squeaky clean and dry after my evening shower.

It's important to break up the Camino by picking a day or two to rest. My brother and I originally picked Burgos and León, before I left the Camino in 2016. In the winter I chose Ponferrada because I wanted to tour the Basilica and Knights Templar Castle. I also needed time in Ponferrada to find an outfitter store to replace my shoes.

It's important to change the camera time and date to Spain time before you start the Camino. I also recommend resetting the numbering system to 001. I didn't realize this in 2016 until days into the walk when my combined phone and camera pictures jumbled and mixed up the dates and times. I cannot stress enough the importance to ensure your camera or phone is taking pictures in the highest resolution. It will be disappointing to arrive home to find your pictures blurring when opening them on a computer screen or showing them on a big screen TV.

To charge my camera, MP3 player, Fitbit and phone I brought along a small 2-in-1 dual USB adapter with rapid charge ports. The Motorola® G4 phone had a rapid charge feature which allowed me to charge the phone while eating lunch, thus I did not have to bring a spare battery cell. I brought a six inch charging cord which did not allow me enough length to type emails while the phone was plugged in. I purchased a longer cord in León. I carried a lightweight European socket adapter rather than the heavier worldwide multi-adapter.

Use caution when removing your headphones from your pocket. The black rubber earpieces fell off my headphones more than once when I was removing them from the pack's side pocket. If you are on a road covered in black manure fragments it can take what feels like ages to backtrack and find a stray earpiece.

I wore Gore-Tex® gaiters each and every day, rain or shine. The primary reason was to keep mud and snow out of my shoes and keep my pant legs clean. But even when the weather was good my trekking poles tended to knock pebbles into my shoes, but the gaiters prevented that and saved me from having to stop and empty them.

The trekking poles I used were the non-adjustable Z-pole. I chose them because they are lightweight, strong and break down into thirds to fit inside my pack to carry on the airline. Pick the right length based on body height. Mine were 130cm in length as per a sizing chart, and they fit me well.

I bought a shampoo bar from Lush. It was lightweight and saved me from having to check my pack due to the restrictions on liquids. I also used the bar to wash my clothes. I'm still using it to wash my hair, weeks after the Camino.

Avoid resting too long during the walk and make sure to stretch your legs throughout the day. This will help to keep soreness from setting in, and will ease the soreness when you start walking again.

The most important advice I can give to anyone is to be sure to size footwear appropriately to accommodate swelling feet. If you go too large you can always use the heel lock lacing technique. If the shoes are not big enough you risk a trauma that will continue long after the Camino. I lost count of how many concrete Camino markers had shoes placed on top. Rather than being cheeky and littering the Camino with my shoes, I left two pairs of North Face trail runners behind in different albergues with notes offering them for free to the next pilgrim.

Reflections

How do you feel now that it is over? Has the experience changed you? Make any discoveries about yourself? Any lasting, impressions or surprises?

I feel an enormous sense of accomplishment and closure having completed the walk. I do think about the Camino and often think how different the experience would have been had I taken a different route or walked at another time.

One of the ways it's changed me is that I can now correlate my energy levels with being in large groups of people. I discovered I had higher energy levels when I was trekking with fewer pilgrims or alone. This might have to do with my introverted side. I wonder, does an extroverted person experience a draining of energy when walking alone?

The people on the Camino share and genuinely care for you. In Burgos a nice lady stopped her car and got out and walked over to me to point me in the right direction. People shared food along the way. Pilgrims like to compare notes about where they're from, how far they've walked, where they started, and where they are going the next day. More than once I found myself comparing my pilgrim's app with others to see what lodging and services were available at the next stage. I personally enjoyed helping Maurizio find an albergue that would accept his dog.

I learned to trust people and my surroundings. Back home I wouldn't think of walking through some cities in America, let alone at night. I didn't feel that way in Spain. Even when walking by teenagers hanging out on a street corner, I did not feel any threat whatsoever.

I learned that my body is capable of walking far more than my mind thought possible. On the last day I was physically conditioned enough to start walking from Melide at 8:00 a.m. and reach Santiago 53 kilometers later at 8:30 p.m. By this stage of the Camino I was also mentally conditioned to walk that distance.

I did not need much food to walk a near marathon distance each day. If breakfast was not available I did not need much more than a croissant to start the day. I knew there would be a bar or restaurant in an hour or two. I did not stress over food or have any feelings of desperation. I was hungry when I left the municipal albergue in Hospital de la Condesa, but I found a restaurant within a few hours.

It was great to be able to monitor the Fitbit during the Camino so I could track steps and distance. Upon completion, I added up all the screenshots from the Fitbit to see how many steps I had walked. I concluded, by starting from Saint Jean Pied de Port, I walked 1,036,040 steps. There were 479,171 in October 2016 and 556,868 steps in January 2018. The 500-mile walk took 27 days, subtracting my rest day in Ponferrada.

It's been fascinating to see the reactions of people when I share my Camino experience. It has been especially surprising to find that so many people have never even heard of the Camino de Santiago. Something as uneventful as watching a movie, The Way, on an overseas flight set into motion an experience that changed the lives of two brothers. Now we have a closer relationship than ever before.

Also it is interesting to think about the ripple effect, when I look back to see the moment that set my life on a different trajectory. On the flight over to Madrid I happened to wake up from a nap just as a flight attendant was pushing a cart down the aisle. In my peripheral vision I saw a two-year-old sleeping in the aisle with his head about to be run into so I put my arm out and stopped the cart. I held the cart in place until the flight attendant finally looked around to see why I was holding it. I thought to myself, "If I hadn't been on that flight to Spain would the child have been injured?"

One thing that struck me as odd on the Camino was the timing of songs on my MP3 player. For instance, I made a decision to stop walking on the main road west of Hospital de la Condesa and take a short snow-covered path. I hoped the snow would not be too deep and that maybe there would be a restaurant with breakfast over the hill. The short path led me downhill in deep snow and back up another hill before reaching the road again. I was out of breath and sweating profusely and wondered why I hadn't just stuck to the road. Actually, I was worried about getting run over by the passing cars. As I neared the top of the snow-covered hill, a church appeared in front of me, probably built in the 14th century. At that moment "Hallelujah" sung by Jeff Buckley started playing through my headphones.

Another time, a Bette Midler song, "From a Distance," started to play just as I walked over a ridgeline and a valley opened up to snow-covered mountains on the horizon. The song describes distant snow-covered mountains. It was uncanny. These two emotional moments were surprising to me, but there were other times when songs seemed to match my environment or situation. When this happened I would look around to see if there was a ray of light shining down on me from a break in the clouds, but I never saw one.

Having lunch with Maurizio on the last day in Santiago

OTHER THINGS

Anything you'd like to talk about that I haven't asked?

Trekking alongside the husky malamute brought me a special joy on the Camino. However, I would discourage taking a dog in winter. There are fewer albergues open in the winter and your chances of finding one that accepts a dog are very slim. As Maurizio said shortly after leaving Hontanas, "Nanook walks the same miles I do, and he too needs proper rest and cannot sleep outside." Maurizio and I maintained contact with each other on WhatsApp throughout the walk. I later met him at the cathedral square when he arrived in Santiago de Compostela—the finale of his three-month journey from Rome. Seeing the joy on his face and the excitement in Nanook, will stay with me for the rest of my life. We had lunch later that afternoon and he explained how difficult it was to walk with a dog in winter. He said to me, "If I walk the Camino again I will not bring the dog." He explained there is a well-marked

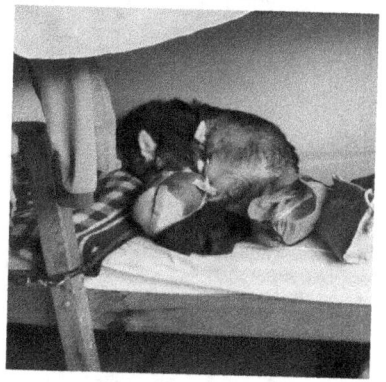

Nanook resting after a long day

southbound Camino in Italy that ends in Rome. But it was difficult to walk the opposite direction from Rome because there are no signs or markers to point the way. He said there were no open albergues in the winter months in Italy and the cost to stay with a dog in a hotel was very expensive.

I haven't felt that alive in a long time. There was the excitement and adventure on the trail not knowing what spectacle is around each corner. I walked through every possible climate zone, including forest, desert, marshland, tundra, and sub-arctic climates. I embraced the physical, mental, emotional and spiritual stages on the Camino. Understanding that my Camino begins after finishing the walk to Santiago, part of the responsibility as a pilgrim for me is to now enlighten and encourage others to the Way of Saint James.

I was privileged to have had the opportunity to host the Camino Amigos ABQ, Albuquerque Chapter of American Pilgrims on the Camino, at a potluck dinner in my home to share my experience. This is a fantastic group of people with a love for and a wealth of knowledge of the Camino. I enjoyed giving a presentation and showing pictures from my winter Camino. I am also honored and thankful to be asked to give this interview.

Packing Checklist

What I packed for the winter walk:

- [ ] Osprey Stratos 36 pack
- [ ] Reflector for back of pack
- [ ] REI Magma 850 Down Jacket
- [ ] Marmot® Super Mica Rain Jacket
- [ ] Marmot® PreCip Full Zip Pant
- [ ] 2 pair prAna Men's Brion Inseam Pants
- [ ] Columbia® polyester long sleeve shirt
- [ ] 3 pair REI Midweight Merino Wool Hiking Crew Socks
- [ ] 3 pair Injinji® Liner Crew Socks
- [ ] REI Merino Midweight Half-Zip Base Layer Top
- [ ] REI Merino Midweight Half-Zip Base Layer Bottoms
- [ ] 3 ExOfficio Give-N-Go Sport Mesh Boxer Briefs 9 inch Inseam

- ☐ 1 pair The North Face GTX Trail-Running Shoes (Gore-Tex®) I left these in Leon because they were not large enough.
- ☐ 1 pair Superfeet® Premium Insoles
- ☐ 1 pair knee sleeves (soft brace)
- ☐ 1 pair flip-flops (shower shoes)
- ☐ NEMO Nocturne 15° Sleeping Bag (-9 C deg 700-fill duck down).
- ☐ 1 pair Black Diamond Gore-Tex® Gaiters
- ☐ 1 pair Black Diamond Distance Carbon Z Trekking Poles 130 cm
- ☐ wide brim hat
- ☐ handkerchief
- ☐ 1 pair fleece gloves
- ☐ Anker PowerPort AC Power Adapter 2 USB with Quick Charge 3.0
- ☐ European socket adapter
- ☐ Motorola G4 unlocked with Quick Charge 3.0
- ☐ Nikon Coolpix S9900 with built-in Wi-Fi
- ☐ MP3 player with two sets of headphones
- ☐ headlamp with lithium batteries
- ☐ small keychain flashlight
- ☐ 1 pair earplugs
- ☐ Platypus 3L water reservoir
- ☐ bottle of Fizz electrolyte tablets
- ☐ box of ibuprofen

- [ ] fleece hat, gloves, and ear muffs
- [ ] microfiber travel towel
- [ ] Lush Shampoo Bar
- [ ] Dr. Bronner's soap bar (cut in half)
- [ ] travel size Gold Bond medicated foot powder
- [ ] SPF ChapStick, sunscreen, and other toiletries
- [ ] first aid items, Band-Aids, antibiotic ointment, and needle
- [ ] Camino de Santiago Maps: St. Jean Pied de Port–Santiago de Compostela paperback by John Brierley
- [ ] scallop shell on lanyard

Items purchased in Ponferrada:

- [ ] Outdoor Research Whitefish Hat—which had ear muffs and a hidden face mask in a zippered pocket for super cold temps. It not only kept the sun out of my eyes it was very warm and breathable.
- [ ] Outdoor Research Shuck Mitt— which I wore over my fleece gloves to keep the wind and rain out.
- [ ] The North Face Endurus Hike Boots, with Vibram® soles.
- [ ] meter long USB charging cord for cell phone.

Useful Phone Apps

Buen Camino—Pilgrim's App published by Editorial Buen Camino SL.

Google Translate—Uses the camera to translate signs written in Spanish, useful for deciphering the historical markers along the way. It will translate languages between two people providing the microphone is close enough to hear the words.

WhatsApp—You'll find yourself communicating with other pilgrims on the Camino. It works great to phone family and friends back home for free.

Fitbit—Step tracker to calculate actual distance walked and calories burned.

Nikon App—To sync with phone and for the transfer large-sized pictures via Wifi.

The Weather Channel—Provided reliable weather and temperature information.

www.ingramcontent.com/pod-product-compliance
Lightning Source LLC
Chambersburg PA
BHW051953290426
0CB00015B/2220